LOOK!

by Ted Lewin

I
Like to
Read®

Holiday House / New York

For Gaby, who loves books

I LIKE TO READ is a registered trademark of Holiday House, Inc.

Copyright © 2013 by Ted Lewin
All Rights Reserved
HOLIDAY HOUSE is registered in the U.S. Patent and Trademark Office.
Printed and Bound in October 2012 at Tien Wah Press, Johor Bahru, Johor, Malaysia.
The text typeface is Report School.
The artwork was created with pencil and watercolor on Strathmore bristol.
www.holidayhouse.com
First Edition
1 3 5 7 9 10 8 6 4 2

Library of Congress Cataloging-in-Publication Data
Lewin, Ted.
Look! / Ted Lewin. — 1st ed.
p. cm. — (An I like to read)
Summary: "An elephant eats, giraffes drink, a warthog digs, and
a boy plays, reads, and dreams."— Provided by publisher.
ISBN 978-0-8234-2607-2 (hardcover)
1. Animals—Africa—Juvenile literature. 2. Animal ecology—Africa—Juvenile literature. I. Title.
QL49.L3875 2013
590.22'2—dc23
2011049607

Look!

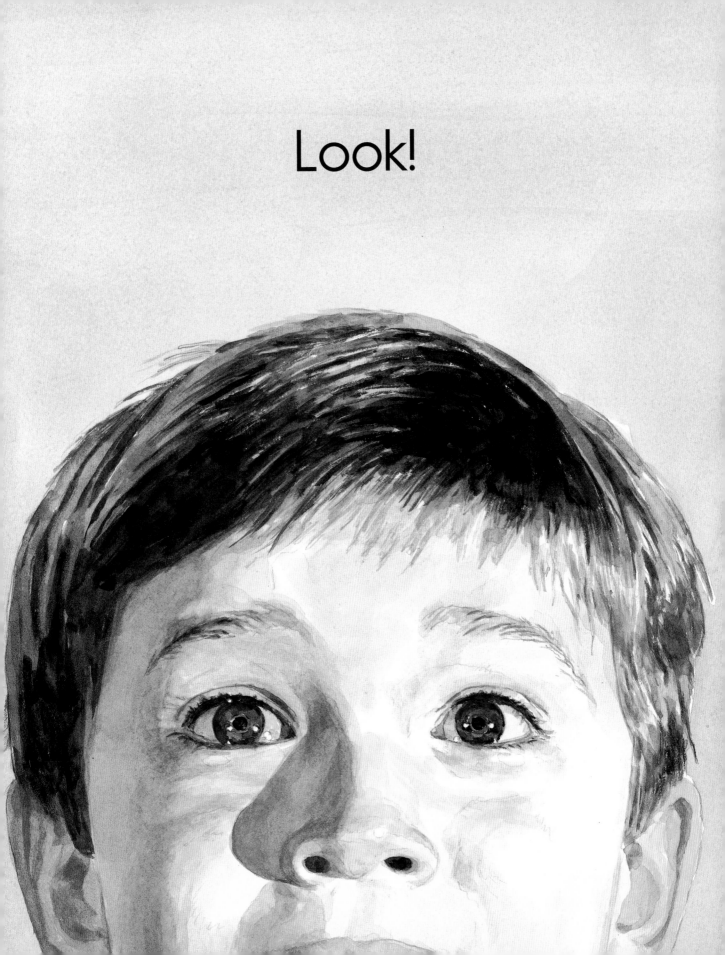

Look! An elephant eats.

Look! Giraffes drink.

Look! A warthog digs.

Look! A gorilla hides.

Look! Wild dogs listen.

Look!

Zebras run.

Look! Monkeys sit.

Look! Hippos splash.

Look! A rhino naps.

Look! A boy plays.

A boy reads.

A boy dreams.